The Christmas Carol Collection

Wise Publications
London/New York/Paris/Sydney/Copenhagen/Madrid

8.95

Contents

Exclusive Distributors:
Music Sales Limited
8/9 Frith Street, London
W1V 5TZ, England.

Music Sales Corporation,
257 Park Avenue South,
New York NY10010,
United States of America.

Music Sales Pty Limited,
120 Rothschild Avenue,
Rosebery, NSW 2018, Australia.

Order No. AM953304
ISBN 0-7119-7772-0
This book © Copyright 1999
by Wise Publications

Music arranged by
Roger Day

Music processed by
Enigma Music Production Services

Cover design by
CDT Design Limited

Printed in the United Kingdom by
Caligraving Limited, Thetford, Norfolk.

Your Guarantee of Quality
As publishers, we strive to produce every book
to the highest commercial standards. The music
has been freshly engraved and the book has been
carefully designed to minimise awkward page
turns and to make playing from it a real pleasure.

Particular care has been given to specifying acid-free,
neutral-sized paper made from pulps which have
not been elemental chlorine bleached. This pulp is
from farmed sustainable forests and was produced
with special regard for the environment. Throughout,
the printing and binding have been planned to
ensure a sturdy, attractive publication which should
give years of enjoyment. If your copy fails to meet
our high standards, please inform us and we
will gladly replace it.

Music Sales' complete catalogue describes
thousands of titles and is available in full colour
sections by subject, direct from Music Sales
Limited. Please state your areas of interest and
send a cheque/postal order for £1.50 for postage
to: Music Sales Limited, Newmarket Road,
Bury St. Edmunds, Suffolk IP33 3YB.

www.internetmusicshop.com

A Virgin Most Pure

Traditional

Folk style

1. A__ vir - gin__ most__ pure, as the

pro - -phets do tell. Hath_ brought_ forth_ a_

ba - by, as it hath be - fa. To be our Re -

-deem - er from death, Hell_ and sin which_

Verse 2:
At Beth'lem in Jewry a city there was
Where Joseph and Mary together did pass
And there to be taxed with many one mo'
For Caesar commanded the same should be so.

Aye and therefore *etc.*

Verse 3:
But when they had entered the city so fair
A number of people so mighty was there
That Joseph and Mary whose substance was small
Could find in the inn there no lodging at all.

Aye and therefore *etc.*

Verse 4:
Then were they constrained in a stable to lie
Where horses and asses they used for to tie.
Their lodging so simple they took it no scorn
But against the next morning our Saviour was born.

Aye and therefore *etc.*

Verse 5:
The King of all kings to this world being brought
Small store of fine linen to wrap Him was sought
And when she had swaddled her young Son so sweet
Within an ox manger she laid Him to sleep.

Aye and therefore *etc.*

Verse 6:
Then God sent an angel from heaven so high
To certain poor shepherds in fields where they lie
And bade them no longer in sorrow to stay
Because that our Saviour was born on this day.

Aye and therefore *etc.*

Verse 7:
Then presently after the shepherds did spy
A number of angels that stood in the sky
They joyfully talked and sweetly did sing
To God be all glory, our heavenly King.

Aye and therefore *etc.*

All My Heart This Night Rejoices

Words by Paulus Gerhardt
Music by Johann Ebeling
English Words by Catherine Winkworth

Verse 2:
Hark, a voice from yonder manger
Soft and sweet, doth entreat, "Flee from woe and danger!
Brethren come from all that grieves you!
You are freed, all your need I will surely give you."

Verse 3:
Come then, let us hasten yonder
Here let all, great and small, kneel in awe and wonder.
Love Him who with love is yearning
Hail the star that from afar bright with hope is burning.

Verse 4:
Blessed Saviour, let me find Thee
Keep thou me, close to Thee, cast me not behind Thee!
Life of life, my heart Thou stillest
Calm I rest on Thy breast, all this Thou fillest.

All Through The Night

Traditional

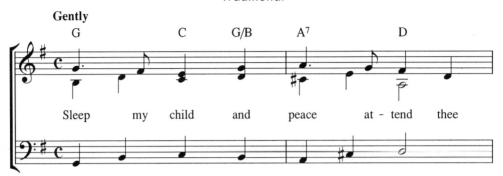

Sleep my child and peace at - tend thee

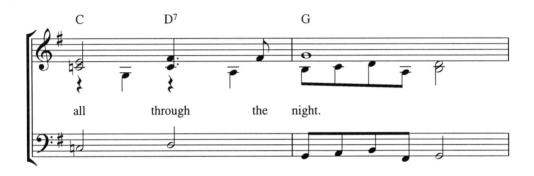

all through the night.

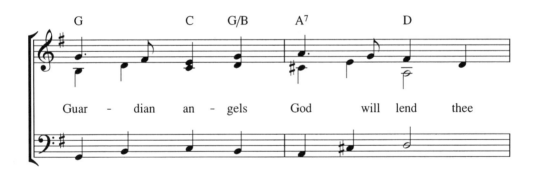

Guar - dian an - gels God will lend thee

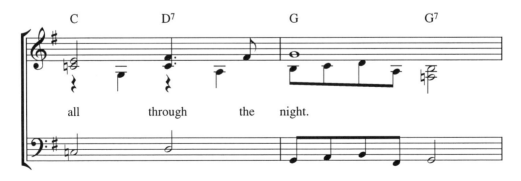

all through the night.

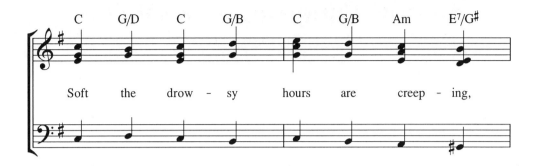

Soft the drow - sy hours are creep - ing,

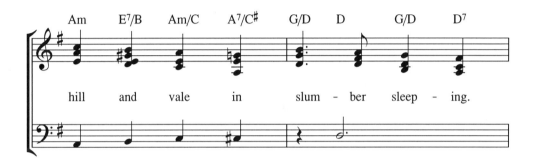

hill and vale in slum - ber sleep - ing.

Love a - lone His watch is keep - ing

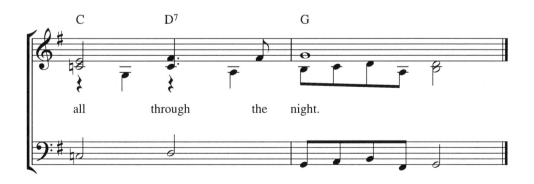

all through the night.

As With Gladness, Men Of Old

Words by William Dix
Music by Conrad Kocher

Moderately

1. As with gladness, men of old. Did the guiding star behold. As with joy they hail'd its light, leading onward, beaming bright. So, most gracious Lord, may we evermore be led by Thee!

Verse 2:
As with joyful steps they sped
To that lowly manger bed,
There to bend the knee before
Him whom heaven and earth adore.
So may we with willing feet
Ever seek Thy mercy seat.

Verse 3:
As they offered gifts most rare
At that manger rude and bare
So may we with holy joy
Pure and free from sin's alloy.
All our costliest treasurer bring
Christ to Thee, our heav'nly King.

Verse 4:
Holy Jesus, every day
Keep us in the narrow way
And when earthly things are past
Bring our ransomed souls at last,
Where they need no star to guide
Where no clouds Thy glory hide.

Away In A Manger

Traditional

1. A-way in a manger, no crib for a

bed, the little Lord Je-sus laid down His sweet

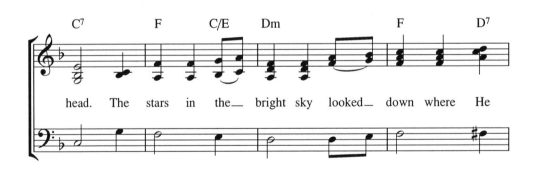

head. The stars in the bright sky looked down where He

lay, the little Lord Je-sus a-sleep on the hay.

Verse 2:
The cattle are lowing
The Baby awakes
But Little Lord Jesus
No crying He makes.
I love Thee, Lord Jesus
Look down from the sky
And stay by my side
Until morning is nigh.

Verse 3:
Be near me, Lord Jesus
I ask Thee to stay
Close by me forever
And love me, I pray.
Bless all the dear children
In Thy tender care
And fit us for heaven
To live with Thee there.

Angels From The Realms Of Glory

Traditional

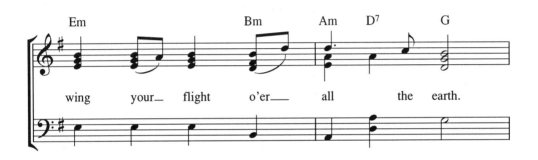

CHORUS

Come___
Glo - - - - - - - - - -

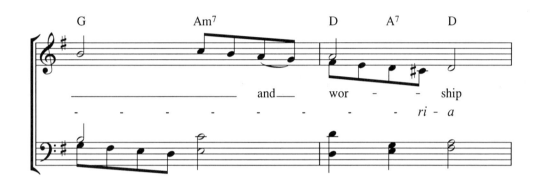

_____ and___ wor - - ship
- - - - - - - - - - ri - a

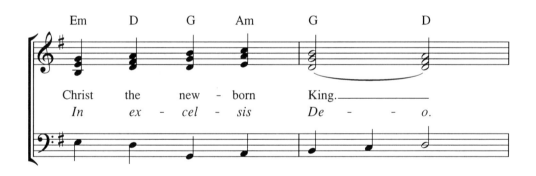

Christ the new - born King.___
In ex - cel - sis De - - o.

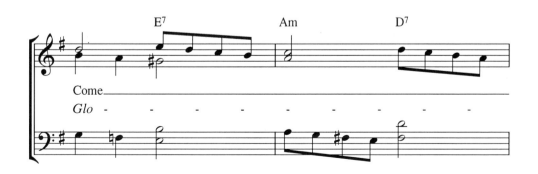

Come___
Glo - - - - - - - - - -

and____ wor - - ship
- - - - - - - - ri - a

wor - ship Christ the new - - born King.
in ex - cel - sis De - - - o.

Verse 2:
Shepherds in the field abiding
Watching o'er your flocks by night.
God with man is now residing
Yonder shines the infant Light

Come and worship *etc.*

Verses 3:
Sages, leave your contemplations
Brighter visions beam afar.
Seek the great Desire of nations
Ye have seen His natal star.

Come and worship *etc.*

Verse 4:
Saints before the alter bending
Watching long in hope and fear.
Suddenly the Lord descending
In His temple shall appear.

Come and worship *etc.*

Verse 5:
Though an infant now we view Him
He shall fill His Father's throne.
Gather all the nations to Him
Every knee shall then bow down.

Come and worship *etc.*

Carol Of The Drum

Words & Music by Katherine Davis

Moderato

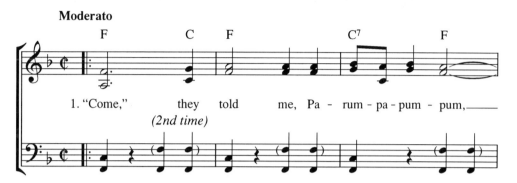

1. "Come," they told me, Pa - rum - pa - pum - pum,___
(2nd time)

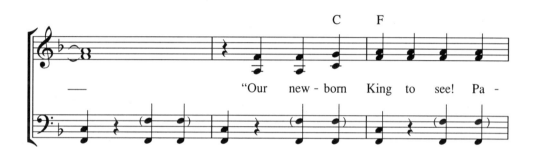

___ "Our new - born King to see! Pa -

- rum - pa - pum - pum,___ Our fin - est

gifts we'll bring, Pa - rum - pa - pum - pum,___

To lay be - fore the King! Pa - rum-pa-pum-pum,

Rum-pa-pum-pum, Rum-pa-pum - pum,_____

So to hon - our Him, Pa - rum-pa-pum - pum,_____

_____ When_ we come."_____

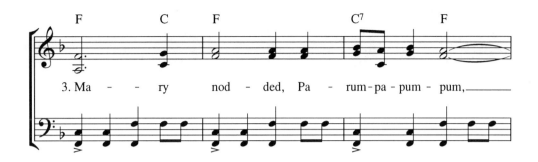

3. Ma - - ry nod - ded, Pa - rum-pa-pum - pum,_____

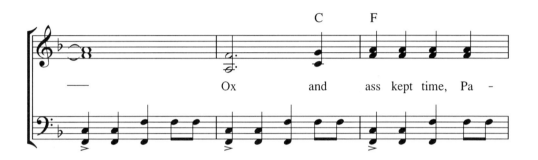

_____ Ox and ass kept time, Pa -

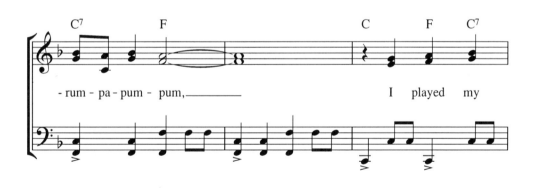

- rum - pa - pum - pum,_____ I played my

drum for Him, Pa - rum - pa-pum - pum,_____

I played my best for Him, Pa - rum - pa - pum - pum,

Rum - pa - pum - pum, Rum - pa - pum - pum,

N.C.

Then He smiled at me, Pa -

- rum - pa - pum - pum!_____ Me and my drum!_____

N.C.

Verse 2:
"Baby Jesu, Pa rum pa pum pum,
I'm a poor boy too, Pa rum pa pum pum,
I have no gifts to bring, Pa rum pa pum pum,
That's fit to give a King, Pa rum pa pum,
Rum pa pum pum, Rum pa pum pum,
Shall I play for you, Pa rum pa pum pum,
On my drum?"

Child In The Manger

Traditional Melody
Words by Mary MacDonald

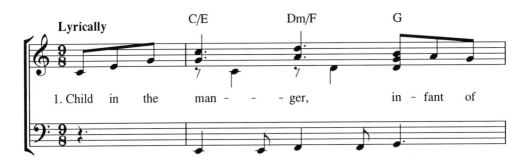

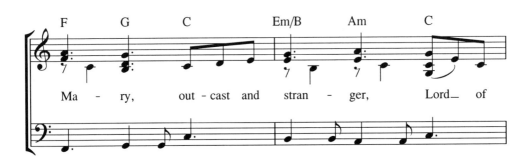

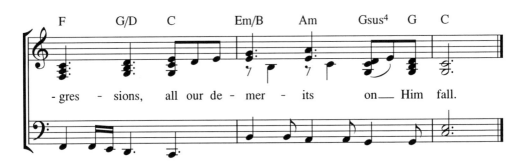

Verse 2:
Once the most holy Child of salvation
Gently and lowly lived below.
Now as our glorious mighty Redeemer
See Him victorious o'er each foe.

Verse 3:
Prophets foretold Him, Infant of wonder
Angels behold Him on His throne.
Worthy our Saviour of all their praises
Happy for ever are His own.

Christians Awake

Traditional

With movement

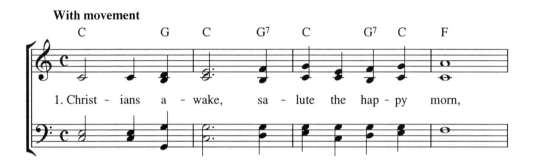

1. Christ - ians a - wake, sa - lute the hap - py morn,

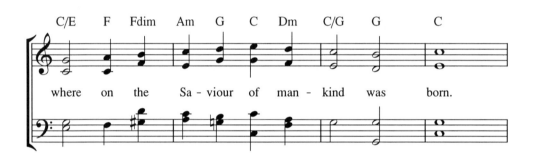

where on the Sa - viour of man - kind was born.

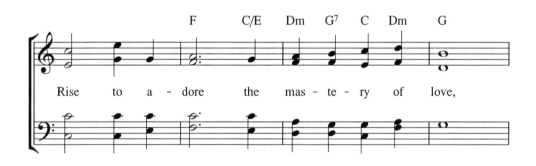

Rise to a - dore the mas - te - ry of love,

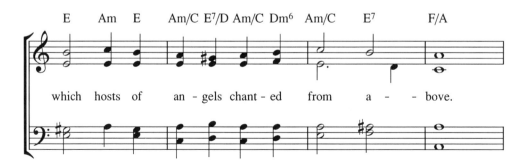

which hosts of an - gels chant - ed from a - - bove.

With them the joy - ful ti - dings first be - gun. Of

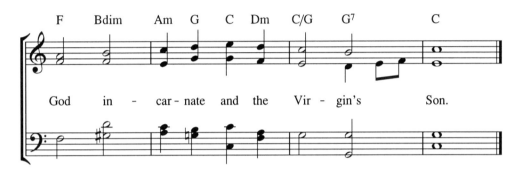

God in - car - nate and the Vir - gin's Son.

Verse 2:
Then to the watchful shepherds it was told
Who heard th'angelic herald's voice "Behold!
I bring good tidings of a Saviour's birth
To you and all the nations upon earth.
This day hath God fulfilled His promised word.
This day is born a Saviour; Christ the Lord!"

Verse 3:
He spake and straightaway the celestial choir
In hymns of joy, unknown before conspire.
The praises of redeeming love they send
And heaven's whole arch with alleluias rang.
God's highest glory was their anthem still,
Peace upon earth and unto men goodwill.

Verse 4:
To Bethl'hem straight the happy shepherds ran
To see the wonder God had wrought for man.
And found with Joseph and the Blessed Maid
Her Son, the Saviour, in a manger laid.
Amazed, the wond'rous story they proclaim
The earliest heralds of the Saviour's name.

Christ Was Born On Christmas Day

Traditional

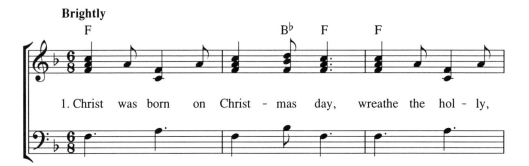

1. Christ was born on Christ - mas day, wreathe the hol - ly,

twine the bay, *Chris - tus na - tus ho - di - e* the

babe the Son the Ho - ly one of Ma - ry.

Verse 2:
He is born to set us free.
He is born our Lord to be.
Ex maria virgine
Our God, our Lord, by all adorned forever.

Verse 3:
Let the bright berries glow
Everywhere in goodly show
Christus natus hodie
The babe, the Son, the Holy One of Mary.

Verse 4:
Christian men rejoice and sing
'Tis the birthday of a King
Ex Maria virgine
The God, the Lord, by all adorned forever.

Christmas Is Coming

Traditional

In a jolly mood

1. Christ - mas is com - ing! The goose is get - ting fat!

Please to put a pen - ny in an old man's— hat!

Please to put a pen - ny in an old man's hat!

Verse 2:
If you've no penny, a ha'penny will do
If you have no ha'penny then God bless you!
If you have no ha'penny then God bless you!

Come, Come, Come To The Manger

Traditional

Come, come, come to the man - ger, chil - dren come to the

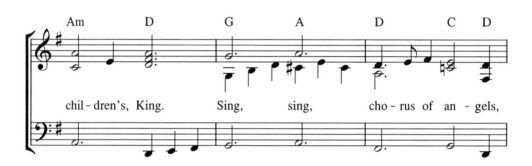

chil - dren's, King. Sing, sing, cho - rus of an - gels,

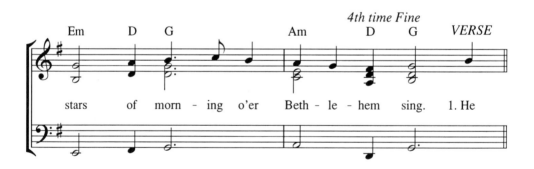

stars of morn - ing o'er Beth - le - hem sing. 1. He

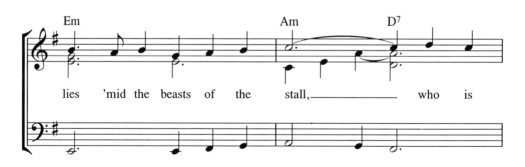

lies 'mid the beasts of the stall, _____ who is

Ma - ker and Lord of us all. _____ The win - try wind blows

cold and drea - ry, see, He weeps_ the world is wea - ry.

a tempo

Lord have pi - ty and mer - cy on me.

Verse 2:
He leaves all His glory behind
To be born and to die for mankind
With grateful beasts His cradle chooses
Thankless man His love refuses.
Lord, have pity and mercy on me!

Come, come, *etc.*

Verse 3:
To the manger of Bethlehem come
To the Saviour Emmanuel's home.
The heav'nly hosts above are singing
Set the Christmas bells a'ringing.
Lord, have pity and mercy on me!

Come, come, *etc.*

Deck The Halls

Traditional

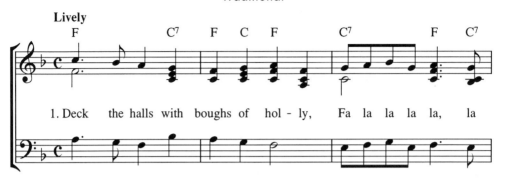

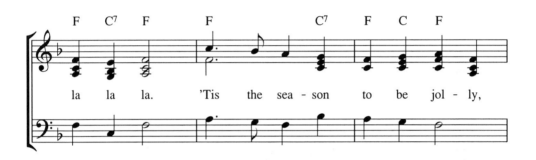

Troll the an-cient Yule-tide ca-rol, Fa la la la la, la la la la.

Verse 2:
See the blazing Yule before us
Fa la la la la, la la la la
Strike the harp and join the chorus
Fa la la la la, la la la la
Follow me in merry measure
Fa la la, fa la la, la la la
While I tell of Yuletide pleasure
Fa la la la la, la la la la.

Verse 3:
Fast away the old year passes
Fa la la la la, la la la la
Hail the new, ye lads and lasses
Fa la la, fa la la, la la la
Sing we joyous all together
Fa la la la la, la la la la
Heedless of the wind and weather
Fa la la la la, la la la la.

Ding Dong Merrily On High

Traditional

Lively

1. Ding dong mer - ri - ly on high   in heav'n the bells are ring - ing.

Ding dong ve - ri - ly the sky   is riv'n with an - gels sing - ing.

Glo - - - - - - -

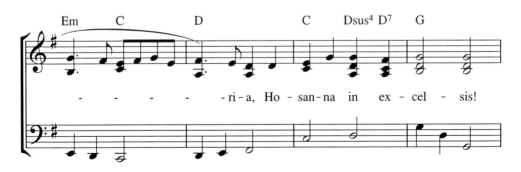

- - - - - ri - a, Ho - san - na in ex - cel - sis!

Verse 2:
Ding dong carol all the bells
Ring out the Christmas story.
Ding dong sound the good nowells
God's Son has come in glory.

Gloria Hosanna in excelsis!
Gloria Hosanna in excelsis!

Verse 3:
Praise Him! People far and near
And join the angels' singing.
Ding dong everywhere we hear
The Christmas bells a' ringing.

Gloria Hosanna in excelsis!
Gloria Hosanna in excelsis!

Verse 4:
Hear them ring this happy morn
Our god a gift has given.
Ding dong Jesus Christ is born
A precious Child from heaven.

Gloria Hosanna in excelsis!
Gloria Hosanna in excelsis!

Go, Tell It On The Mountain

Traditional

Bright spiritual

CHORUS

Go, tell it on the moun - tain, ov - er the hills and

ev - 'ry - where.— Go, tell it on the moun - tain, our

Je - sus Christ— is born. *Fine* *VERSE* 1. While shep - herds kept their

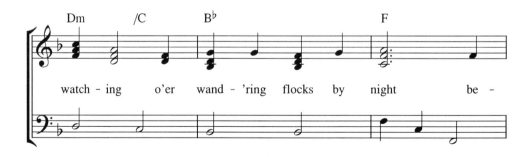

watch - ing o'er wand - 'ring flocks by night be -

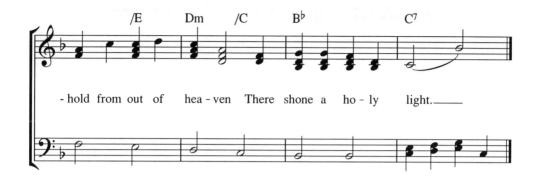

/E Dm /C B♭ C⁷

- hold from out of hea - ven There shone a ho - ly light._____

Verse 2:
And lo, when they had seen it
They all bowed down and prayed
They travelled on together
To where the babe was laid.

Go, tell *etc.*

Verse 3:
When I was a seeker
I sought both night and day
I asked my Lord to help me
And He showed me the way.

Go, tell *etc.*

Verse 4:
He made me a watchman
Upon the city wall
And if I am a Christian
I am the least of all.

Go, tell *etc.*

God Rest Ye Merry, Gentlemen

Traditional

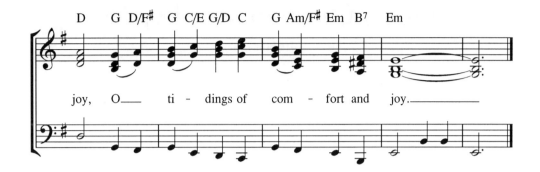

joy, O—— ti - dings of com - fort and joy.————

Verse 2:
From God our heavenly Father
A blessed angel came
And unto certain shepherds
Brought tidings of the same
How that in Bethlehem was born
The Son of God by name.

O tidings of comfort *etc.*

Verse 3:
"Fear not, then" said the angel
"Let nothing you affright.
This day is born a Saviour
Of virtue, power and might.
So frequently to vanquish all
The friends of Satan quite."

O tidings of comfort *etc.*

Verse 4:
The Shepherds at those tidings
Rejoiced much in mind
And left their flocks a' feeding
In tempest, storm and wind
And went to Bethlehem straight away
This blessed Babe to find

O tidings of comfort *etc.*

Verse 5:
But when to Bethlehem they came
Whereat this Infant lay
They found Him in a manger
Where oxen feed on hay.
His mother Mary kneeling
Unto the Lord did pray

O tidings of comfort *etc.*

Verse 6:
Now to the Lord sing praises
All ye within this place
And with true love and brotherhood
Each other now embrace.
This holy tide of Christmas
All other doth deface.

O tidings of comfort *etc.*

Good Christian Men Rejoice

Traditional

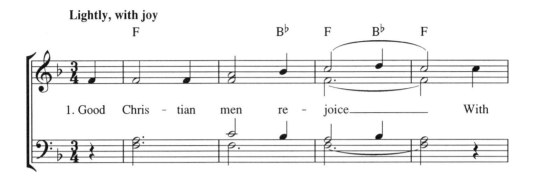

Lightly, with joy

1. Good Chris - tian men re - joice_____ With

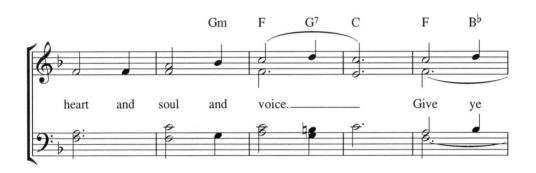

heart and soul and voice._____ Give ye

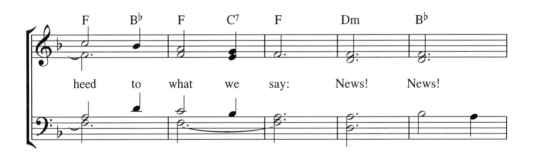

heed to what we say: News! News!

Je - - sus Christ is born to - day.

Ox and ass be - fore Him bow, He is

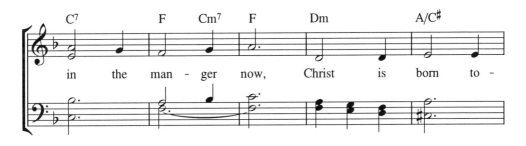

in the man - ger now, Christ is born to -

- day,_____ Christ is born to - day._____

Verse 2:
Good Christian men, rejoice
With heart and soul and voice.
Now ye hear of endless bliss
Jesus Christ was born for this.

He hath op'n'd the heav'nly door
And man is blessed for ever more
Christ was born for this
Christ was born for this!

Verse 3:
Good Christian men, rejoice
With heart and soul and voice
Now ye need not fear the grave
Jesus Christ was born to save.

Calls you one and calls you all
To gain His everlasting hall.
Christ was born to save
Christ was born to save!

Good King Wenceslas

Traditional

Moderately

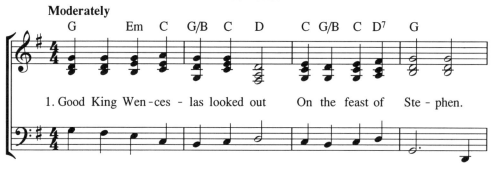

1. Good King Wen-ces-las looked out   On the feast of   Ste-phen.

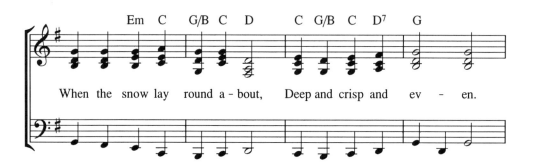

When the snow lay   round a-bout,   Deep and crisp and   ev   -   en.

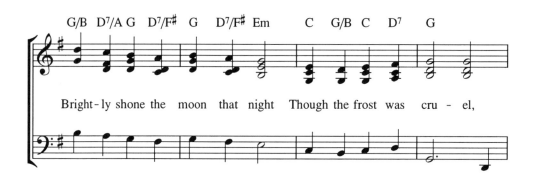

Bright-ly shone the   moon that night   Though the frost was   cru - el,

When a poor man came in sight   Gath-'ring win-ter   fu - - el.

Verse 2:

"Hither, page, and stand by me
If thou know'st it telling.
Yonder peasant, who is he?
Where and what his dwelling?"

"Sire, he lives a good league hence
Underneath the mountain.
Right against the forest fence
By St. Agnes' fountain."

Verse 3:

"Bring me flesh and bring me wine
Bring me pine logs hither.
Thou and I will see him dine
When we bear them thither."

Page and monarch forth they went
Onward both together.
Through the rude wind's wild lament
And the bitter weather.

Verse 4:

"Sire, the night is darker now
And the wind blows stronger.
Fails my heart, I know not how
I can go no longer."

"Mark my footsteps, good my page
Tread thou in them boldly.
Thou shalt find the winter's rage
Freeze thy blood less coldly."

Verse 5:

In his master's steps he trod
Where the snow lay dinted.
Heat was in the very sod
Which the saint had printed.

Therefore Christian men be sure
Wealth or rank possessing
Ye who now will bless the poor
Shall yourselves find blessing.

Hark! The Herald Angels Sing

Words by Charles Wesley
Music by Felix Mendelssohn

host pro-claim, Christ is— born in Beth - le - hem.

Hark! The he-rald an-gels sing, glo-ry— to the new-born King.

Verse 2:
Christ by highest heav'n adored
Christ the everlasting Lord.
Late in time, behold Him come
Offspring of a virgin's womb.
Veiled in flesh, the Godhead see!
Hail th'incarnate Deity!
Pleased as man with man to dwell
Jesus, our Immanuel.

Hark the herald *etc.*

Verse 3:
Hail! The heaven born Prince of Peace
Hail! The Son of righteousness
Light and life to all He brings
Risen with healing in His wings.
Mild He lays His glory by
Born that man no more may die
Born to raise the sons of earth
Born to give them second birth.

Hark the herald *etc.*

He Is Born, The Divine Christ Child

(Il Est Né, Le Divin Enfant)

Traditional

Filled with hope, men be-gan to pray, 'Til His com-ing this

hap-py day.— he is born, the di-vine Christ Child.

Greet Him with gai-ly re-sound-ing pipe and drum. He is born, the di-

-vine Christ Child. Join in— song, for the Lord has come.

Here We Come A-Wassailing

Traditional

Verse 2:
Our wassail cup is made of the rosemary tree
And so is your beer of the best barley.

Love and joy *etc.*

Verse 3:
We are not daily beggars that beg from door to door
But we are neighbours' children whom you have seen before.

Love and joy *etc.*

Verse 4:
Call up the butler of this house, put on his golden ring
Let him bring us up a glass of beer and better we shall sing.

Love and joy *etc.*

Verse 5:
We have got a little purse of stretching leather skin
We want a little of your money to line it well within.

Love and joy *etc.*

Verse 6:
Bring us out a table and spread it with a cloth
Bring us out a mouldy cheese and some of your Christmas loaf.

Love and joy *etc.*

Verse 7:
God bless the master of this house, likewise the mistress too
And all the little children that round the table go.

Love and joy *etc.*

Verse 8:
Good master and good mistress while you're sitting by the fire
Pray think of us poor children who are wandering in the mire.

Love and joy *etc.*

I Saw Three Ships

Traditional

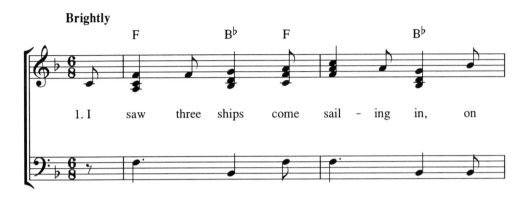

1. I saw three ships come sail - ing in, on

Christ - mas Day,— on Christ - mas Day. I saw three ships come

sail - ing in on Christ - mas Day in the morn - ing.

Verse 2:
And what was in those ships all three
On Christmas Day, on Christmas Day?
And what was in those ships all three
On Christmas Day in the morning?

Verse 3:
Our Saviour Christ and His Lady
On Christmas Day, on Christmas Day
Our Saviour Christ and His Lady
On Christmas Day in the morning

Verse 4:
Pray whither sailed those ships all three
On Christmas Day, on Christmas Day?
Pray whither sailed those ships all three
On Christmas Day in the morning?

Verse 5:
O, they sailed into Bethlehem
On Christmas Day, on Christmas Day
O, they sailed into Bethlehem
On Christmas Day in the morning.

Verse 6:
And all the bells on earth shall ring
On Christmas day, on Christmas Day
And all the bells on earth shall ring
On Christmas Day in the morning.

Verse 7:
And all the angels in heav'n shall sing
On Christmas Day, on Christmas Day
And all the angels in heav'n shall sing
On Christmas Day in the morning.

Verse 8:
And all the souls on earth shall sing
On Christmas Day, on Christmas Day
And all souls on earth shall sing
On Christmas Day in the morning.

Verse 9:
Then let us all rejoice amain
On Christmas Day, on Christmas Day
Then let us all rejoice amain
On Christmas Day in the morning.

In The Bleak Midwinter

Words by Christina Rossetti
Music by Gustav Holst

Verse 2:
Our God, heav'n cannot hold Him
Nor earth sustain
Heav'n and earth shall flee away
When He comes to reign.
In the bleak mid-winter
A stable-place sufficed
The Lord God Almighty
Jesus Christ.

Verse 3:
Angels and archangels
May have gathered there
Cherubim and seraphim
Thronged the air.
But His mother only
In her maiden bliss
Worshipped the Beloved
With a kiss.

Verse 4:
What can I give Him
Poor as I am?
If I were a shepherd
I would bring a lamb.
If I were a wise man
I would do my part.
Yet what can I give Him
Give my heart.

Infant Holy

Traditional Polish Carol
English Words by Edith Reed

1. In-fant ho-ly, In-fant low-ly, for His bed a cat-tle

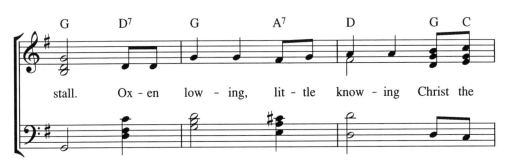

stall. Ox-en low-ing, lit-tle know-ing Christ the

Babe is Lord of all. Swift are wing-ing an-gels

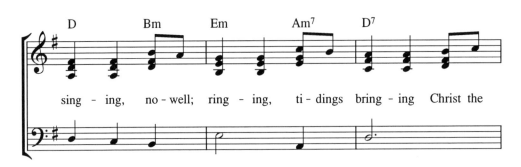

sing-ing, no-well; ring-ing, ti-dings bring-ing Christ the

Babe is Lord of all. Christ the Babe is Lord of all.

Verse 2:
Flocks were sleeping
Shepherds keeping
Vigil till the morning new.
Saw the glory
Heard the story
Tidings of a gospel true.
Thus rejoicing
Free from sorrow
Praises voicing
Greet the morrow.
Christ the Babe was born for you.
Christ the Babe was born for you.

It Came Upon A Midnight Clear

Words by Edmund Hamilton Sears
Music by Richard Storrs Willis

Moderately

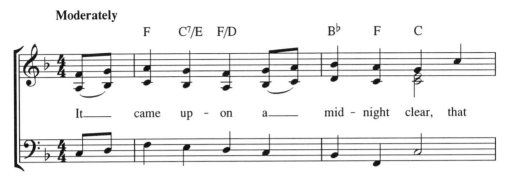

It___ came up - on a___ mid - night clear, that

glo - rious song_ of___ old. From__ an - gels bend - ing

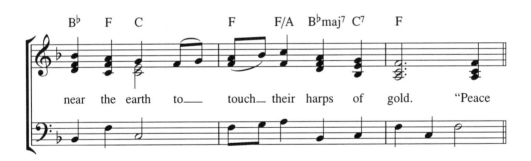

near the earth to___ touch__ their harps of gold. "Peace

on the earth,___ good - will to men from

heav'n's all gra - cious— King." The world in sol - emn

still - ness lay to—— hear— the an - gels sing.

Verse 2:
Still through the cloven skies they come
With peaceful wings unfurled.
And still their heavenly music floats
O'er all the weary world.

Above its sad and lonely plains
They bend on hovering wing.
And ever o'er its Babel sounds
The blessèd angels sing.

Verse 3:
Yet with the woes of sin and strife
The world has suffered long
Beneath the angel-strain have rolled
Two thousand years of wrong.

And man, at war with man, hears not
The love-song which they bring.
O hush the noise, ye men of strife
And hear the angels sing.

Verse 4:
And ye, beneath life's crushing load
Whose forms are bending low
Who toil along the climbing way
With weary steps and slow.

Look up! For glad and golden hours
Come swiftly on the wing.
O rest beside the weary road
And hear the angels sing.

Verse 5:
For Lo! The days are hastening on
By prophet bards foretold
When with ever-circling years
Comes round the Age of Gold.

When peace shall over all the earth
Its ancient splendours fling.
And the whole world give back the song
Which now the angels sing.

Jesus Good Above All Other

Words by Percy Dearmer
Music: Traditional

Verse 2:
Jesus cradled in a manger
For us facing ev'ry danger.
Living as a homeless stranger
Make we Thee our King most dear.

Verse 3:
Jesus for Thy people dying
Risen master, death defying.
Lord in heav'n Thy grace supplying
Keep us to Thy presence near.

Verse 4:
Jesus who our sorrows bearest
All our thoughts and hopes Thou sharest.
Thou to man the truth declarest
Help us all Thy truth to hear.

Verse 5:
Lord, in all our doings guide us
Pride and hate shall ne'er divide us.
We'll go on with Thee beside us
And with joy we'll persevere.

Jingle Bells

Words & Music by J.S. Pierpont

Oh what fun it is to ride in a one horse o-pen sleigh, Hey!

CHORUS

Jin-gle bells jin-gle bells, jin-gle all the way,

Oh what fun it is to ride in a one horse o-pen sleigh.

Verse 2:
Day or two ago
I thought I'd take a ride
Soon Miss Fanny Bright
Was seated at my side.
The horse was lean and lank
Misfortune seemed his lot
He got into a drifted bank
And we, we got upsot.

Jingle bells, *etc.*

Verse 3:
Now the ground is white
Go it while you're young!
Take the girls tonight
And sing this sleighing song.
Just get a bobtail'd bay
Twoforty for his speed
Then hitch him to an open sleigh
And crack! You'll take the lead!

Jingle bells, *etc.*

Joy To The World

Traditional

Steadily, with majesty

1. Joy to the world, the Lord is come. Let

earth re - ceive her King._____ Let

ev - 'ry___ home___ pre - pare___ Him___ room___ and

Heav'n and na - ture___ sing, and___ Heav'n and na - ture sing, and___

Hea - ven and Heav - en and na - ture sing.

Verse 2:
Joy to the world! The Saviour reigns.
Let men their songs employ.
While fields and floods; rocks, hills and plains
Repeat the sounding joy
Repeat the sounding joy
Repeat, repeat the sounding joy.

Verse 3:
No more let sins and sorrows grow
Nor thorns infest the ground.
He comes to make His blessings flow
Far as the curse is found
Far as the curse is found
Far as, far as the curse is found.

Verse 4:
He rules the world with truth and grace
And makes the nations prove.
The glories of His righteousness
And wonders of His love
And wonders of His love
And wonders, and wonders of His love.

Lullaby Carol

Traditional

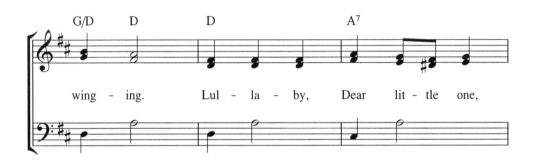

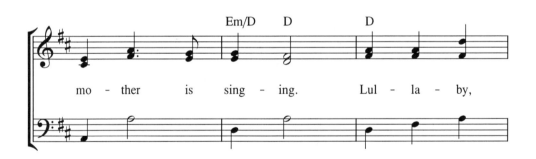

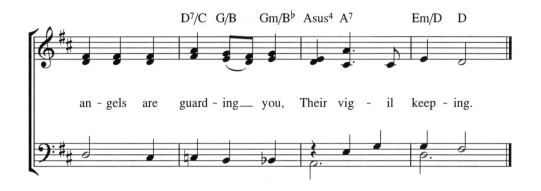

an - gels are guard - ing___ you, Their vig - il keep - ing.

Verse 2:
Lullaby, sweet little one
Sings our dear Lady
Lullaby, sweet little one
To her sweet baby.
Close your eyes, Jesus dear
Hush all your sighing
Mary is guarding you
No need for crying.

Mary Had A Baby

Traditional Afro-American Spiritual

Spiritual, gently

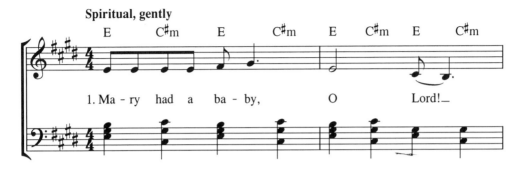

1. Ma - ry had a ba - by, O Lord!__

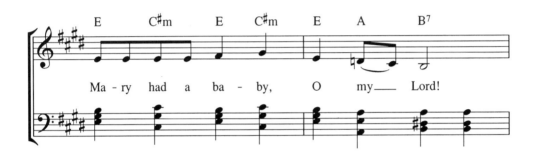

Ma - ry had a ba - by, O my__ Lord!

Ma - ry had a ba - by, O Lord!__ The

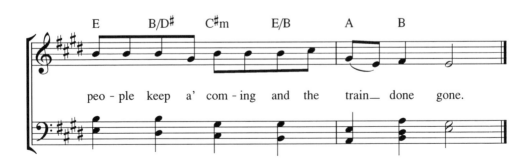

peo - ple keep a' com - ing and the train__ done gone.

Verse 2:
What did she name Him, oh Lord?
What did she name Him, oh my Lord?
What did she name Him, oh Lord?
The people keep a' comin' and the train done gone.

Verse 3:
She called Him Jesus, oh Lord
She called Him Jesus, oh my Lord
She called Him Jesus, oh Lord
The people keep a' comin' and the train done gone.

Verse 4:
Now where was He born, oh Lord?
Where was He born, oh my Lord?
Where was He born, oh Lord?
The people keep a' comin' and the train done gone.

Verse 5:
Born in a stable, oh Lord
Born in a stable, oh my Lord
Born in a stable, oh Lord
The people keep a' comin' and the train done gone.

Verse 6:
Where did they lay Him, oh Lord?
Where did they lay Him, oh my Lord?
Where did they lay Him, oh Lord
The people keep a' comin' and the train done gone.

Verse 7:
Laid Him in a manger, oh Lord
Laid Him in a manger, oh my Lord
Laid Him in a manger, oh Lord
The people keep a' comin' and the train done gone.

continued

Verse 8:
Who came to see Him, oh Lord?
Who came to see Him, oh my Lord?
Who came to see Him, oh Lord?
The people keep a' comin' and the train done gone.

Verse 9:
Shepherds came to see Him, oh Lord
Shepherds came to see Him, oh my Lord
Shepherds came to see Him, oh Lord
The people keep a' comin' and the train done gone.

Verse 10:
The wise men kneeled before Him, oh Lord
The wise men kneeled before Him, oh my Lord
The wise men kneeled before Him, oh Lord
The people keep a' comin' and the train done gone.

Verse 11:
King Herod tried to find Him, oh Lord
King Herod tried to find Him, oh my Lord
King Herod tried to find Him, oh Lord
The people keep a' comin' and the train done gone.

Verse 12:
They went away to Egypt, oh Lord
They went away to Egypt, oh my Lord
They went away to Egypt, oh Lord
The people keep a' comin' and the train done gone.

Verse 13:
Angels watching over Him, oh Lord
Angels watching over Him, oh my Lord
Angels watching over Him, oh Lord
The people keep a' comin' and the train done gone.

Masters In This Hall

Words by William Morris
Music: Traditional

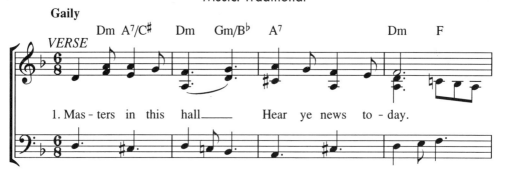

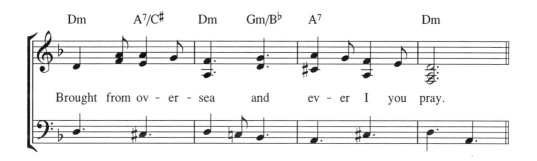

No-well, no-well, no - well, no-well sing we loud! God to -

- day hath all folk raised— and—— cast a' down the proud.

Verse 2:
Going o'er the hills through the milk white snow
Heard I ewes bleat while the wind did blow.

Nowell, nowell, *etc.*

Verse 3:
Shepherds many an one sat among the sheep
No man spake more than had they been asleep.

Nowell, nowell, *etc.*

Verse 4:
Quoth I, "Fellows mine, why this guise sit ye?
Making but dull cheer, shepherds though be ye."

Nowell, nowell, *etc.*

Verse 5:
"Shepherds should of right leap and dance and sing
Thus to see ye sit is a right strange thing

Nowell, nowell, *etc.*

Verse 6:
Quoth these fellows then, "To Bethlehem we go
To see a mighty Lord lie in manger low."

Nowell, nowell, *etc.*

Verse 7:
"How name ye this Lord, shepherds?" Then said I.
"Very God," they said, "Come from heaven high."

Nowell, nowell, *etc.*

Verse 8:
Then to Bethl'em town we went two and two
And in a sorry place heard the oxen low.

Nowell, nowell, *etc.*

Verse 9:
Therein did we see a sweet and goodly may
And a fair old man. Upon the straw she lay.

Nowell, nowell, *etc.*

Verse 10:
And a little child on her arm had she
"What ye who this is?" Said the hinds to me.

Nowell, nowell, *etc.*

Verse 11:
Ox and ass we know, kneeling on their knee
Wond'rous joy had I, this little babe to see.

Nowell, nowell, *etc.*

Verse 12:
This is Christ the Lord! Masters be ye glad!
Christmas is come in and no folk should be sad.

Nowell, nowell, *etc.*

O Christmas Tree

Traditional

Moderately, steady beat

1. O Christ - mas tree,_____ O Christ - mas tree,_____ How
true you stand, un - chang - ing. O Christ - mas tree,_____ O
Christ - mas tree,_____ How true you stand, un - -
- chang - ing. Your boughs so green___ in sum - mer time___ re -

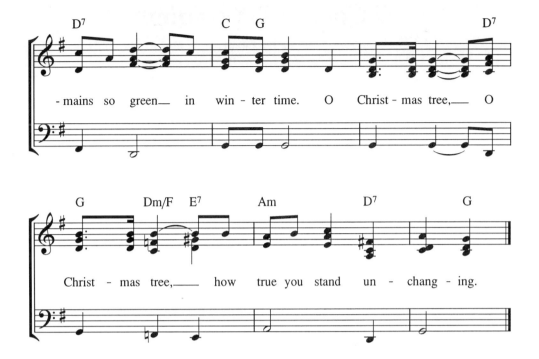

- mains so green— in win - ter time. O Christ - mas tree,— O
Christ - mas tree,— how true you stand un - chang - ing.

Verse 2:
O christmas tree, O Christmas tree
Thy message is enduring.
O Christmas tree, O Christmas tree
Thy message is enduring.
So long ago in Bethlehem
Was born the Saviour of all men.
O Christmas tree, O Christmas tree
Thy message is enduring!

Verse 3:
O Christmas tree, O Christmas tree
Thy faith also unchanging.
O Christmas tree, O Christmas tree
Thy faith also unchanging.
A symbol sent from God above
Proclaiming Him the Lord of love!
O Christmas tree, O Christmas tree
How true you stand unchanging!

O Come All Ye Faithful

Words & Music by John Francis Wade
English Words by Frederick Oakeley

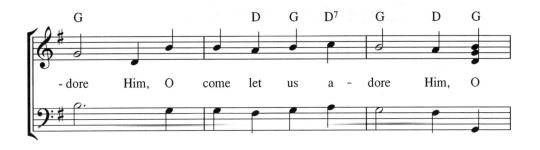

-dore Him, O come let us a - dore Him, O

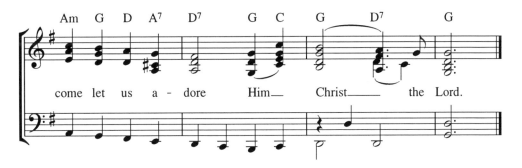

come let us a - dore Him— Christ— the Lord.

Verse 2:
God of God
Light of Light
Lo, He abhors not the Virgin's womb!
Very God
Begotten, not created.

O come let us *etc.*

Verse 3:
Sing, choirs of angels
Sing in exultation!
Sing all ye citizens of heav'n above!
Glory to God
In the highest!

O come let us *etc.*

Verse 4:
Yea, Lord, we greet Thee
Born this happy morning
Jesus, to Thee be glory giv'n!
Word of the Father
Now in flesh appearing.

O come let us *etc.*

O Come, O Come Emmanuel

Traditional

With feeling

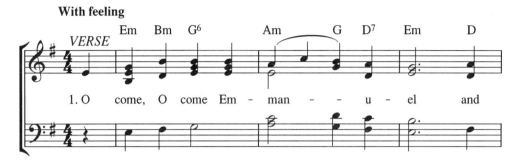

VERSE
1. O come, O come Em - man - u - el and

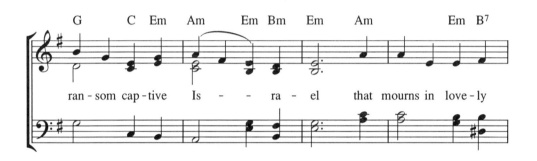

ran - som cap - tive Is - ra - el that mourns in love - ly

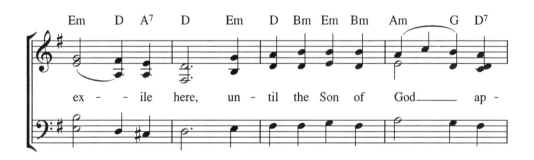

ex - ile here, un - til the Son of God___ ap -

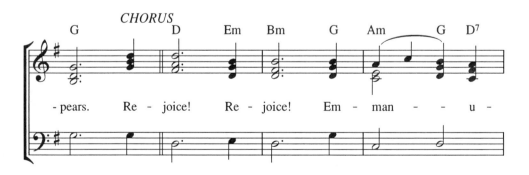

CHORUS
- pears. Re - joice! Re - joice! Em - man - u -

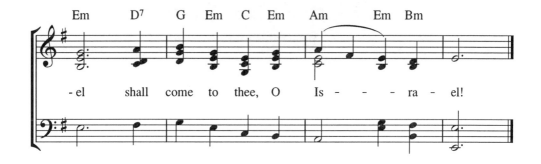

-el shall come to thee, O Is - - - ra - el!

Verse 2:
O come, o come, Thou Lord of might
Who to Thy tribes on Sinai's height.
In ancient times didst give law
In cloud and majesty and awe.

Rejoice! Rejoice! *etc.*

Verse 3:
O come Thou rod of Jesse
Free Thine own from Satan's tyranny.
From depths of hell Thy people save
And give them victory o'er the grave.

Rejoice! Rejoice! *etc.*

Verse 4:
O come, Thou dayspring, come and cheer
Our spirits by Thine advent here.
Disperse the gloomy clouds of night
And death's dark shadows put to flight.

Rejoice! Rejoice! *etc.*

Verse 5:
O come, Thou key of David come
And open wide our heav'nly home.
Make safe the way that leads on high
And close the path to misery.

Rejoice! Rejoice! *etc.*

O Little One Sweet
(O Jesulein Süss)

Words by Samuel Scheidt
Music by Johann Sebastian Bach
English Words by Percy Dearmer

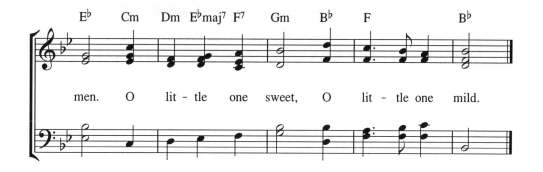

men. O lit - tle one sweet, O lit - tle one mild.

Verse 2:
O little one sweet, O little one mild
With joy thou hast the whole world filled.
Thou camest here from heav'n's domain
To bring men comfort in their pain.
O little one sweet, O little one mild.

Verse 3:
O little one sweet, O little one mild
In thee love's beauties are all distilled.
Then light in us thy love's bright flame
That we may give thee back the same
O little one sweet, O little one mild.

Verse 4:
O little one sweet, O little one mild
Help us to do as thou hast willed.
Lo, all we have belongs to thee
Ah, keep us in our fealty!
O little one sweet, O little one mild.

O Little Town Of Bethlehem

Words by Phillips Brooks
Music by Lewis Redner

Moderately

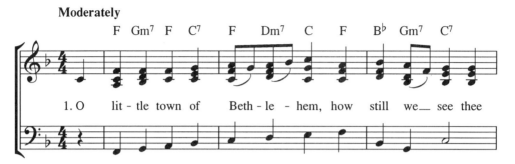

1. O lit - tle town of Beth - le - hem, how still we__ see thee

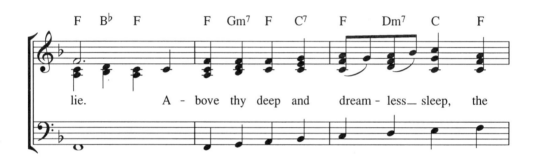

lie. A - bove thy deep and dream - less__ sleep, the

si - lent__ stars go by. Yet__ in thy dark__ streets__

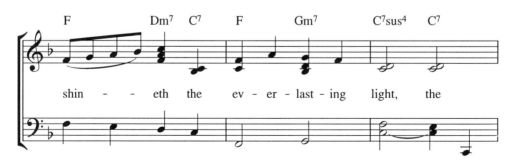

shin - - eth the ev - er - last - ing light, the

hopes and fears of all— the—years are met in— thee to - night.

Verse 2:
O morning stars together
Proclaim the Holy birth.
And praises sing to God the King
And peace to men on earth!
For Christ is born of Mary
And gathered all above
While mortals sleep the angels keep
Their watch of wond'ring love.

Verse 4:
How silently, how silently
The wond'rous gift is given.
So God imparts to human hearts
The blessings of His heaven.
No ear may hear His coming
But in this world of sin
Where meek souls will receive Him, still
The dear Christ enters in.

Verse 5:
Where children pure and happy
Pray to the blessèd Child.
Where misery cries out to Thee
Son of the mother mild.
Where charity stands watching
And faith holds wide the door
The dark night wakes, the glory breaks
And Christmas comes once more.

Verse 6:
O holy Child of Bethlehem
Descend to us, we pray.
Cast out our sin and enter in
Be born in us today.
We hear the Christmas angels
The great glad tidings tell
O come to us, abide with us
Our Lord Emmanuel.

Once In Royal David's City

Words by Cecil Alexander
Music by Henry Gauntlett

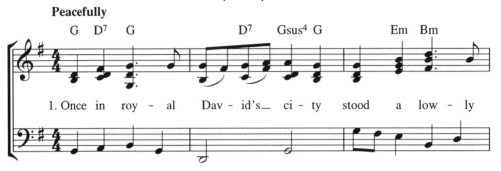

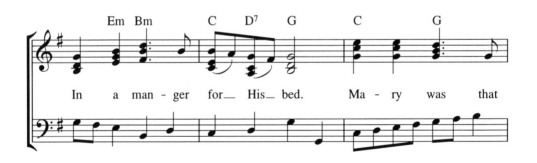

Verse 2:

He came down to earth from heaven
Who is God and Lord of all.
And His shelter was a stable
And His cradle was a stall.
With the poor and mean and lowly
Lived on earth our Saviour holy.

Verse 3:

And through all His wond'rous childhood
He would honour and obey
Love and watch the lowly mother
In whose gentle arms He lay.
Christian children all must be
Mild, obedient, good as He.

Verse 4:

For He is our childhood's pattern
Day by day, like us He grew.
He was little, weak and helpless
Tears and smiles, like us He knew.
And He feeleth for our sadness
And He shareth in our gladness.

Verse 5:

And our eyes at last shall see Him
Through His own redeeming love.
For that Child so dear and gentle
Is Our Lord in heaven above.
And He leads His children on
To the place where He is gone.

Verse 6:

Not in that poor lowly stable
With the oxen standing by.
We shall see Him, but in heaven
Set at God's right hand on high.
Where like stars His children crowned
All in white shall wait around.

Rejoice And Be Merry

Traditional

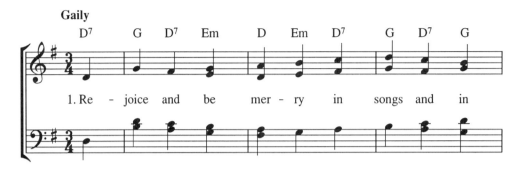

1. Re - joice and be mer - ry in songs and in

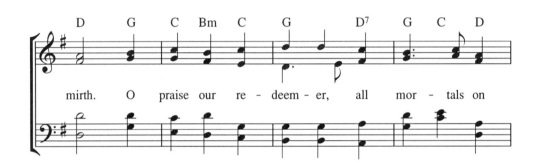

mirth. O praise our re - deem - er, all mor - tals on

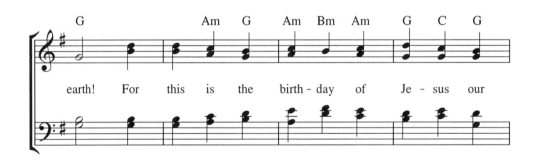

earth! For this is the birth - day of Je - sus our

King, who brought us sal - va - tion, His prais - es we'll sing!

Verse 2:
A heavenly vision appeared in the sky
Vast numbers of angels, the shepherds did spy.
Proclaiming the birthday of Jesus our King
Who brought us salvation, His praises we'll sing.

Verse 3:
Likewise a bright star in the sky did appear
Which led the wise men from the East to draw near.
They found the Messiah, sweet Jesus our King
Who brought salvation, His praises we'll sing.

Verse 4:
And when they were come, they their treasures unfold
And unto Him offered myrrh, incense and gold.
So blessèd for ever be Jesus our King
Who brought us salvation, His praises we'll sing.

Rise Up Shepherd

Traditional

Spiritual, with fervour

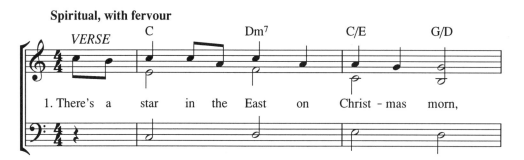

VERSE
1. There's a star in the East on Christ-mas morn,

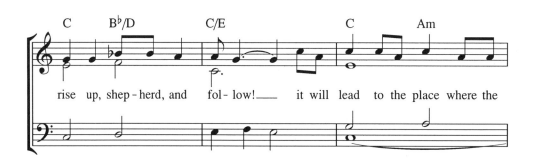

rise up, shep-herd, and fol-low! it will lead to the place where the

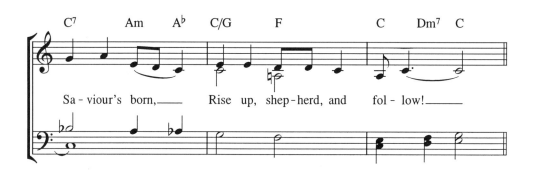

Sa-viour's born, Rise up, shep-herd, and fol-low!

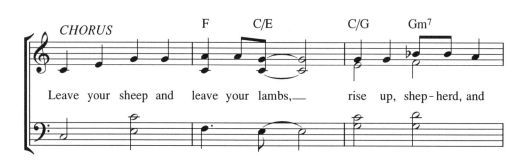

CHORUS
Leave your sheep and leave your lambs, rise up, shep-herd, and

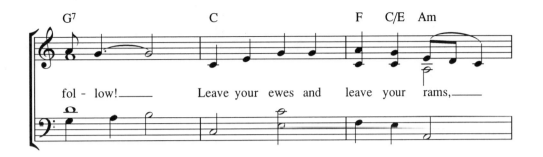

fol - low!___ Leave your ewes and leave your rams,___

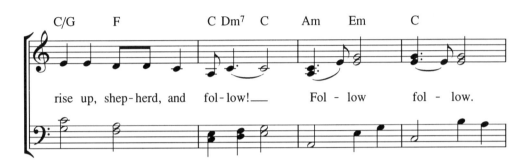

rise up, shep-herd, and fol-low!___ Fol - low fol - low.

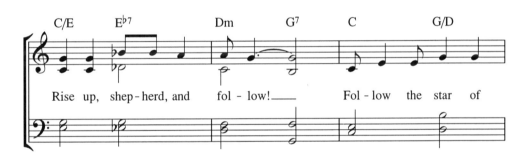

Rise up, shep-herd, and fol - low!___ Fol - low the star of

Beth - le - hem,___ rise up, shep - herd, and fol - low.___

Verse 2:
If you take good heed to the angel's words
Rise up, shepherd, and follow!
You'll forget your flocks, you'll forget your herds
Rise up, shepherd, and follow!

Leave your sheep*etc.*

Rocking

Traditional Czech Carol

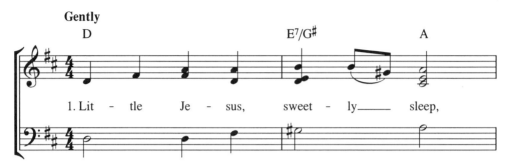

1. Lit - tle Je - sus, sweet - ly____ sleep,

do not___ stir, we will___ lend a____ coat of___ fur.

We will rock you, rock you. rock___ you. We will rock you,

rock you, rock____ you. See the fur to

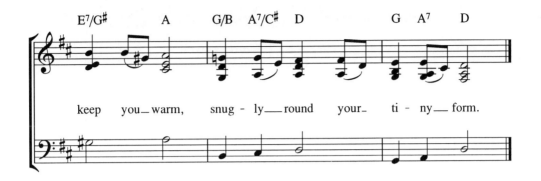

keep you— warm, snug - ly—round your— ti - ny— form.

Verse 2:
Mary's little baby, sleep
Sweetly sleep
Sleep in comfort, slumber deep.
We will rock you, rock you, rock you
We will rock you, rock you, rock you.
We will serve you all we can
Darling, darling, little man.

See Amid The Winter's Snow

Words by Edward Caswall
Music by John Goss

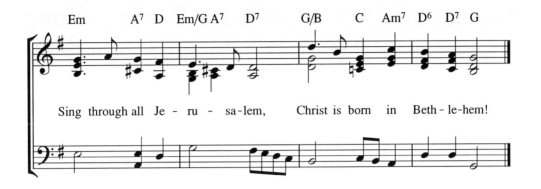

Sing through all Je - ru - sa-lem, Christ is born in Beth - le-hem!

Verse 2:
Lo, within a manger lies
He who built the starry skies.
He, who throned in height sublime
Sits amid the cherubim.

Hail thou ever *etc.*

Verse 3:
Say, ye holy shepherds say
What your joyful news today.
Wherefore have ye left your sheep
On the lonely mountain steep?

Hail thou ever *etc.*

Verse 4:
As we watched at dead of night
Lo, we saw a wond'rous light.
Angels singing peace on earth
Told us of the Saviour's birth.

Hail thou ever *etc.*

Verse 5:
Sacred Infant, all divine
What a tender love was Thine.
Thus to come from highest bliss
Down to such a world as this!

Hail thou ever *etc.*

Verse 6:
Teach, o teach us, Holy Child
By Thy face so meek and mild.
Teach us to resemble Thee
In Thy sweet humility.

Hail thou ever *etc.*

Shepherds! Shake Off Your Drowsy Sleep

Traditional

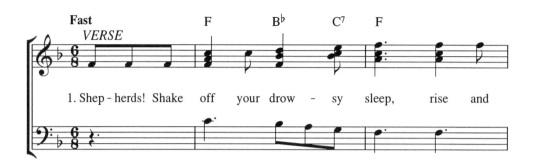

1. Shep-herds! Shake off your drow-sy sleep, rise and

leave your sil-ly sheep. An-gels from heav'n a-round loud

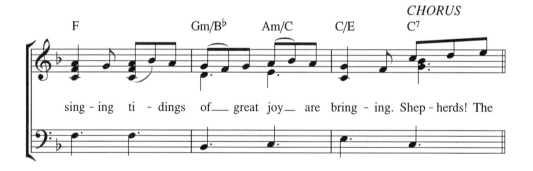

sing-ing ti-dings of great joy are bring-ing. Shep-herds! The

chor-us come and swell, sing No-el, o sing No-el.

Verse 2:
Hark! Even now the bells ring round
Listen to their merry sound.
Hark how the birds new songs are making
As if winter's chains were breaking.

Shepherds! The *etc.*

Verse 3:
See how the flow're all burst anew
Thinking snow is summer dew.
See how the stars afresh are glowing
All their brightest beams bestowing.

Shepherds! The *etc.*

Verse 4:
Cometh at length the age of peace
Strife and sorrow now shall cease
Prophets foretold the won'drous story
Of this heav'n-born Prince of glory

Shepherds! The *etc.*

Verse 5:
Shepherds then up and quick away
Seek the Babe ere break of day
He is the hope of every nation
All in Him shall find salvation

Shepherds! The *etc.*

Silent Night

Words by Joseph Mohr
Music by Franz Gruber

Sleep   in   hea - ven - ly   peace,_____

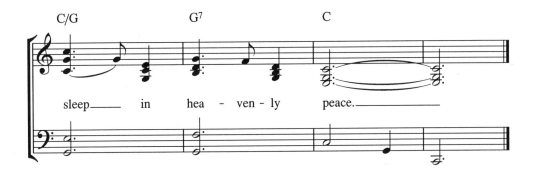

sleep____   in   hea - ven - ly   peace._____

Verse 2:
Silent night, Holy night.
Shepherds quake at the sight
Glories stream from heaven afar
Heav'nly hosts sing Alleluia.
Christ, the Saviour is born
Christ, the Saviour is born.

Verse 3:
Silent night, Holy night.
Son of God, love's pure light.
Radiant beams from Thy holy face
With the dawn of redeeming grace.
Jesus Lord at Thy birth
Jesus Lord at Thy birth.

Sussex Carol

Traditional

news of our mer - ci - ful___ King's birth.___

Verse 2:
Then why should men on earth be so sad
Since our Redeemer made us glad?
Then why should men on earth be so sad
Since our Redeemer made us glad?
When from our sin He set us free
All for to gain our liberty?

Verse 3:
When sin departs before His grace
Then life and health come in its place.
When sin departs before His grace
Then life and health come in its place.
Angels and men with joy may sing
All for to see the new-born King.

Verse 4:
All out of darkness we have light
Which made the angels sing this night.
All out of darkness we have light
Which made the angels sing this night.
'Glory to God and peace to men
Now and for evermore. Amen.'

The Angel Gabriel

Words by Sabine Baring-Gould
Music: Traditional

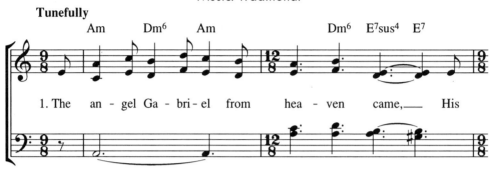

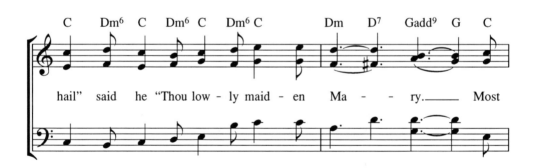

Verse 2:
"For now a blessèd mother thou shalt be
All generations laud and honour thee.
Thy Son shall be Emmanuel, by seers foretold.
Most highly favour'd lady. Gloria!"

Verse 3:
Then gentle Mary meekly bowed her head
"To me be as it pleaseth God," she said.
"My soul shall laud and magnify His holy name."
Most highly favour'd lady. Gloria!

Verse 4:
Of her, Emmanuel the Christ was born
In Bethlehem, all on a Christmas morn.
And Christian folk throughout the world will ever say
"Most highly favour'd lady. Gloria!"

The Boar's Head Carol

Traditional

Verse 2:
The boar's head as I understand
The bravest dish in all the land.
When thus bedecked with a gay garland
Let us servire cantico.
(Let us serve with song.)

Caput apri etc.

Verse 3:
Our steward hath provided this
In honour of the King of bliss
Which on this day to be served is
In regimensi atrio.
(In the royal hall.)

Caput apri etc.

The Cherry Tree Carol

Traditional

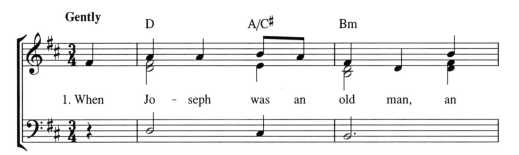

1. When Jo - seph was an old man, an

old man was he. He___ mar - ried vir - gin

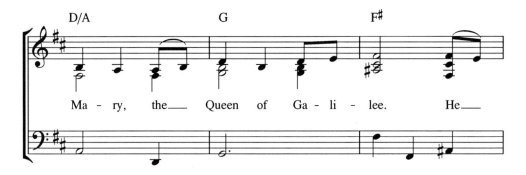

Ma - ry, the___ Queen of Ga - li - lee. He___

mar - ried vir - gin Ma - ry, the___ Queen of Ga - li - lee.

Verse 2:
When Joseph and Mary
Walked through an orchard green
There were berries and cherries as thick as might be seen
There were berries and cherries as thick as might be seen.

Verse 3:
And Mary spoke to Joseph
So meek and so mild
"Joseph, gather me some cherries for I am with child.
Joseph, gather me some cherries for I am with child."

Verse 4:
And Joseph flew in anger
In anger flew he
"Let the father of the baby gather cherries for thee.
Let the father of the baby gather cherries for thee."

Verse 5:
Then up spoke baby Jesus
From in Mary's womb
"Bend down the tallest tree that my mother might have some.
Bend down the tallest tree that my mother might have some."

Verse 6:
And bent down the tallest branch
Till it touched Mary's hand
Cried she, "O, look thou Joseph, I have cherries by command."
Cried she, "O, look thou Joseph, I have cherries by command."

The Coventry Carol

Traditional

Moderately

CHORUS

Lul - ly lul - la Thou lit - tle ti - ny child,

By by lul - ly lu - - lay. 1. O sis - ters

too, how may we do for to pre -

- serve this day This poor young - ling for

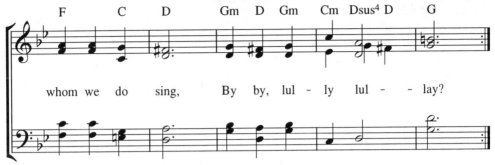

Verse 2:
Herod the king in his raging
Chargèd he hath this day.
His men of might, in his own sight
All young children to slay.

Verse 3:
That woe is me, poor child for Thee!
And ever morn and day
For thy parting neither say nor sing
By by, lully lullay!

Lully lulla *etc.*

The First Nowell

Traditional

Gently

CHORUS

deep. No - well,___ No - well, No - well No -

- well, born is the King___ of Is - - ra - el.

Verse 2:
They lookèd up and saw a star
Shining in the east, beyond them far.
And to the earth it gave great light
And so it continued both day and night.

Nowell Nowell, *etc.*

Verse 3:
And by the light of that same star
Three wise men came from country far.
To seek for a king was their intent
And to follow the star wherever it went.

Nowell Nowell, *etc.*

Verse 4:
This star drew nigh to the north-west
O'er Bethlehem it took its rest.
And there it did both stop and stay
Right over the place where Jesus lay.

Nowell Nowell, *etc.*

Verse 5:
Then entered in those wise men three
Full rev'rently upon their knee.
And offered there in His presence
Their gold and myrrh and frankincence

Nowell Nowell, *etc.*

Verse 6:
Then let us all with one accord
Sing praises to our heavenly Lord.
That hath made heaven and earth of nought
And with His blood mankind hath bought.

Nowell Nowell, *etc.*

The Holly And The Ivy

Traditional

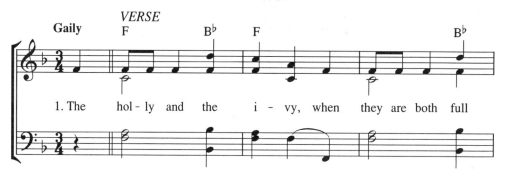

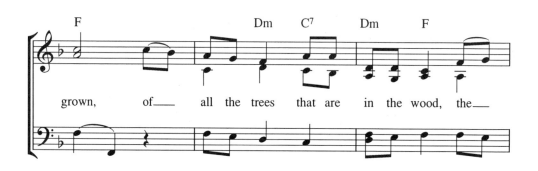

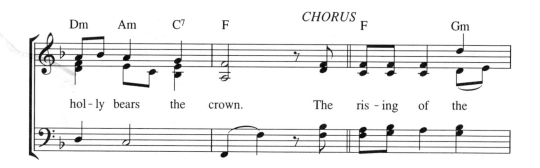

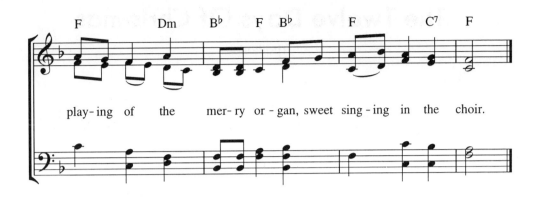

play-ing of the mer-ry or-gan, sweet sing-ing in the choir.

Verse 2:
The holly bears a blossom
As white as the flow'r
And Mary bore sweet Jesus Christ
To be our sweet Saviour.

The rising of *etc.*

Verse 3:
The holly bears a berry
As red as any blood
And Mary bore sweet Jesus Christ
To do poor sinners good.

The rising of *etc.*

Verse 4:
The holly bears a prickle
As sharp as any thorn
And Mary bore sweet Jesus Christ
On Christmas Day in the morn.

The rising of *etc.*

Verse 5:
The holly bears a bark
As bitter as any gall
And Mary bore sweet Jesus Christ
For to redeem us all.

The rising of *etc.*

Verse 6:
The holly and the ivy
When they are both full grown
Of all the trees that are in the wood
The holly bears the crown.

The rising of *etc.*

The Twelve Days Of Christmas

Traditional

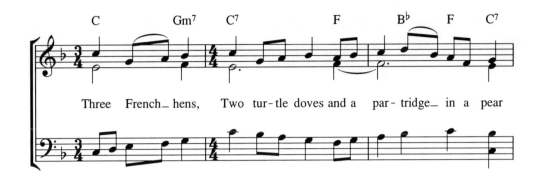

Three French— hens, Two tur-tle doves and a par-tridge— in a pear

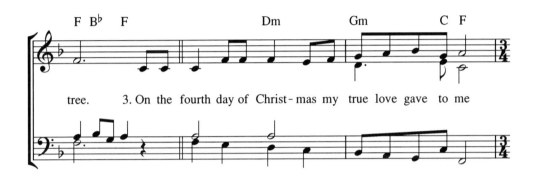

tree. 3. On the fourth day of Christ-mas my true love gave to me

Four call-ing birds, Three French— hens, Two tur-tle doves, and a

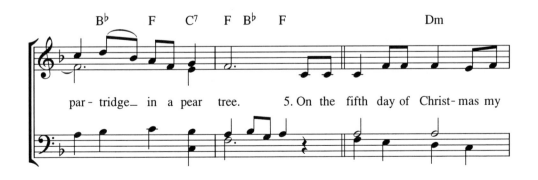

par-tridge— in a pear tree. 5. On the fifth day of Christ-mas my

true love gave to me   Five   gol - den   rings,

Four___   call - ing   birds,   Three   French   hens,

Two__ tur - tle doves   and a   par - tridge__ in a pear   tree.

6. On   the   sixth   day   of   Christ - mas   my   true love gave to me
7. On   the   seventh   day   of   Christ - mas   my   true love gave to me
8. On   the   eighth   day   of   Christ - mas   my   true love gave to me
9. On   the   ninth   day   of   Christ - mas   my   true love gave to me
10. On   the   tenth   day   of   Christ - mas   my   true love gave to me
11. On   the   eleventh   day   of   Christ - mas   my   true love gave to me
12. On   the   twelfth   day   of   Christ - mas   my   true love gave to me

Six___ geese a - lay - ing, Five gol - den rings,
Sev - en swans a - swim - ming,
Eight___ maids a milk - ing,
Nine___ la - dies wait - ing,
Ten___ lords a - leap - ing,
'Lev - en pip - ers pip - ming,
Twelve_ drum - mers drum - ing,

Four_ call - ing birds, Three French hens, Two_ tur - tle doves, and a

6-11. D. S. 12.
rit.

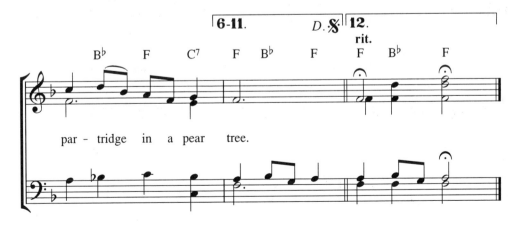

par - tridge in a pear tree.

*Repeat this measure as often as necessary, so that these lines may be sung in reverse order,
each time ending with "Six geese a-laying."

Thou Who Wast Rich

Words by Frank Houghton
Music: Traditional

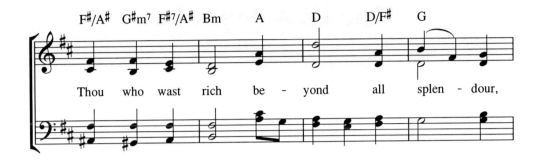

Thou who wast rich be - yond all splen - dour,

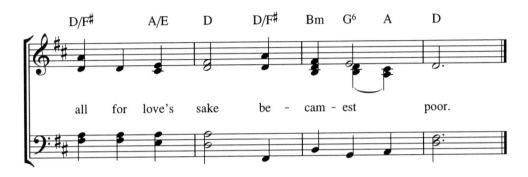

all for love's sake be - cam - est poor.

Verse 2:
Thou who art God beyond all praising
All for love's sake becamest man.
Stooping so low but sinners raising
Heav'nwards by Thine eternal plan.
Thou who art God beyond all praising
All for love's sake becamest man.

Verse 3:
Thou who art love beyond all telling
Saviour and King we worship Thee.
Immanuel within us dwelling
Make us what Thou wouldst have us be.
Thou who art love beyond all telling
Saviour and King we worship Thee.

Unto Us A Boy Is Born

Traditional

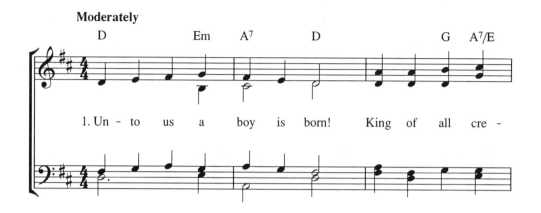

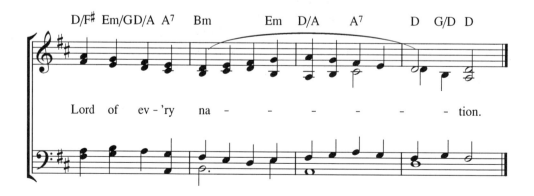

Verse 2:
Cradled in a stall was He
With sleepy cows and asses
But the very beasts could see
That He all men surpasses.

Verse 3:
Herod then with fear was filled
"A prince", he said, "in Jewry!"
All the little boys he killed
At Bethl'em in his fury.

Verse 4:
Now may Mary's son, who came
So long ago to love us
Lead us all with hearts aflame
Unto the joys above us.

Verse 5:
Omega and Alpha He!
Let the organ thunder
While the choir with peals of glee
Doth rend the air asunder.

Torches

Words by J.B. Trend
Music by John Joubert

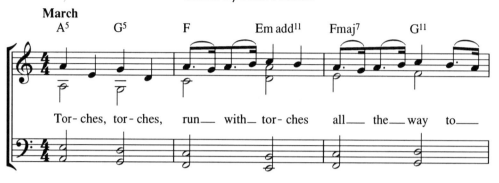

Tor-ches, tor-ches, run— with— tor-ches all— the—way to—

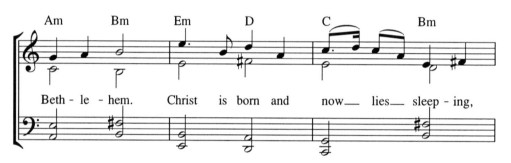

Beth-le-hem. Christ is born and now— lies— sleep-ing,

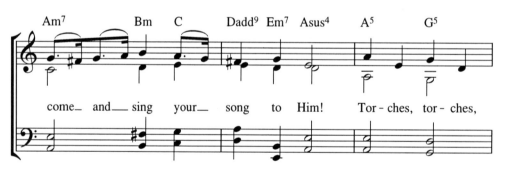

come— and— sing your— song to Him! Tor-ches, tor-ches,

run— with— tor-ches all— the—way to— Beth-le-hem.

118

Em   D   C   Bm   C   G   A⁷

Christ is born and now lies sleep-ing, come and sing your

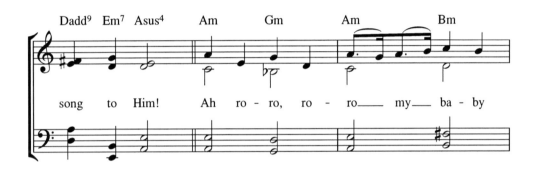

Dadd⁹ Em⁷ Asus⁴   Am   Gm   Am   Bm

song to Him! Ah ro - ro, ro - ro my ba-by

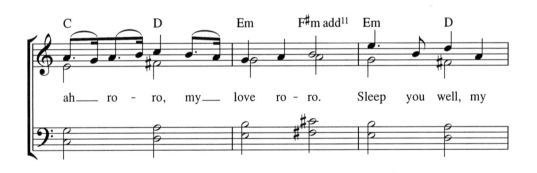

C   D   Em   F♯m add¹¹ Em   D

ah ro - ro, my love ro-ro. Sleep you well, my

C   Bm   C   Bm   Dadd⁹ Em⁷ A⁵

heart's own dar-ling, while we sing you our ro-ro.

While Shepherds Watched

Traditional

1. While shep - herds watched their flocks by night, all seat - ed on the ground. The an - gel of the Lord came down and glo - ry shone a - round.

Verse 2:
"Fear not," said he; for mighty dread
Had seized their troubled mind.
"Glad tidings of great joy I bring
To you and all mankind."

Verse 3:
"To you in David's town this day
Is born of David's line
A Saviour who is Christ the Lord
And this shall be the sign.

Verse 4:
"The heavenly babe you there shall find
To human view displayed
All meanly wrapped in swathing bands
And in a manger laid."

Verse 5:
Thus spake the Seraph and forthwith
Appeared a shining throng
Of angels praising God, who thus
Addressed their joyful song.

Verse 6:
"All glory be to God on high
And on the earth be peace!
Goodwill henceforth from heaven to men
Begin and never cease!"

We Three Kings Of Orient Are

Words & Music by John Henry Hopkins

Moderately

VERSE

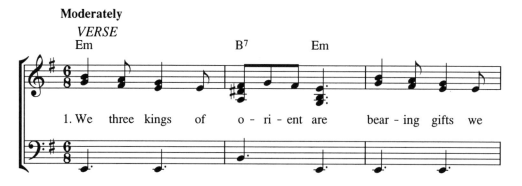

1. We three kings of o - ri - ent are bear - ing gifts we

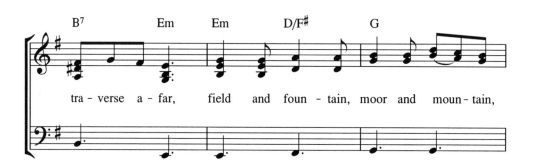

tra - verse a - far, field and foun - tain, moor and moun - tain,

CHORUS

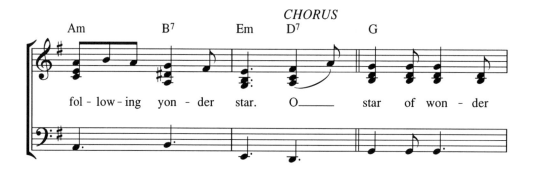

fol - low - ing yon - der star. O____ star of won - der

star of night, star with roy - al beau - ty bright

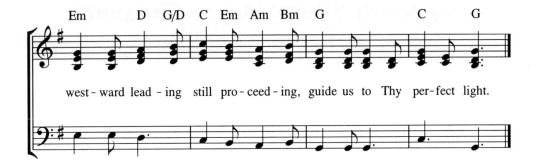

west - ward lead - ing still pro - ceed - ing, guide us to Thy per- fect light.

Verse 2:
Born a King on Bethlehem plain
Gold I bring to crown Him again.
King for ever, ceasing never
Over us all to reign.

O star of wonder *etc.*

Verse 3:
Frankincense to offer have I
Incense owns a Deity nigh.
Prayer and praising, all men raising
Worship Him God most high.

O star of wonder *etc.*

Verse 4:
Myrrh is mine, its bitter perfume
Breathes a life of gathering gloom.
Sorrowing, sighing, bleeding, dying
Sealed in the stone-cold tomb.

O star of wonder *etc.*

Verse 5:
Glorious now, behold Him arise
King and God and Sacrifice!
Heaven sings alleluia
Alleluia the earth replies.

O star of wonder *etc.*

We Wish You A Merry Christmas

Traditional

1. We wish you a mer-ry Christ-mas, we wish you a mer-ry

Christ-mas, we wish you a mer-ry Christ-mas and a hap-py new

year. Good ti-dings we bring to you and your kin. We

wish you a mer-ry Christ-mas and a hap - py new year.

Verse 2:
Now bring us some figgy pudding
Now bring us some figgy pudding
Now bring us some figgy pudding
And bring it out here!

Good tidings *etc.*

Verse 3:
For we all like figgy pudding
For we all like figgy pudding
For we all like figgy pudding
So bring some out here!

Good tidings *etc.*

Verse 4:
And we won't go until we've got some
And we won't go until we've got some
And we won't go until we've got some
So bring some out here!

Good tidings *etc.*

What Child Is This

Traditional

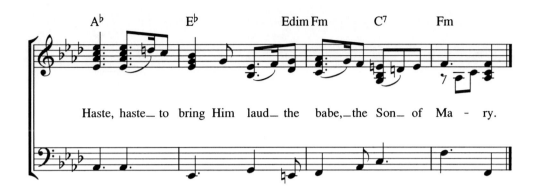

Haste, haste— to bring Him laud— the babe,—the Son— of Ma - ry.

Verse 2:
Why lies He in such mean estate
Where ox and ass are feeding?
Good Christian fear, for sinners here
The silent world is pleading.

Nails, spear shall pierce Him through
The Cross be born, for me, for you
Hail, hail the Word made flesh
The Babe, the Son of Mary.

Verse 3:
So bring Him incense, gold and myrrh
Come peasant king to own Him
The King of kings, salvation brings
Let loving hearts enthrone Him.

Raise, raise the song on high
The virgin sings her lullaby.
Joy, joy for Christ is born
The Babe, the Son of Mary.